FAST FORWARD

Volcano

illustrated by

Peter Dennis

BARRON'S

Contents

Introduction

Imagine you are in southern Italy, and it's thousands of years ago. The scene is dominated by a large volcano blasting ash into the air. One day the eruption will stop and calm will return. Then, many years into the future, the Roman city of Pompeii will be built on the fertile plains beneath that same volcano, known as Vesuvius. The city is a picture of peace and prosperity until one sunny August morning...

The story told in this book is like a journey. It is not a journey you can make by plane, car or ship. In fact, you don't have to go anywhere at all. You are about to travel through time. With each turn of the page, the date moves forward a few hours, days or years. You are still in the same place, but notice how many things change from one date to the next. Each time—each stop on your journey—is like a new chapter. The eruption, the falling pumice and ash, the blast that obliterated the city, the years that passed before the ruins were discovered—all tell the story of Pompeii.

Use this thumb index to travel though time! Just find the page you want to see and flip it open. This way you can make a quick comparison between one scene and another, even though some show events that took place many years apart. A little black arrow on the page points to the time of the scene illustrated on that page.

Vesuvius
erupting

6

25,000 years ago

Europe lies in the grip of the Ice Ages. Vast ice sheets have spread out from the North Pole and the mountain ranges, smothering great expanses of land. Although ice has not come as far as southern Italy, the climate is cool and dry. Few trees grow here. Herds of saiga antelope graze the grasslands.

With a loud explosion, a volcano (which will one day be known as Vesuvius) erupts, blasting ash into the air. Alarmed by the shaking ground and deafening noise, the saiga gallop away, blocks of lava crashing all around them.

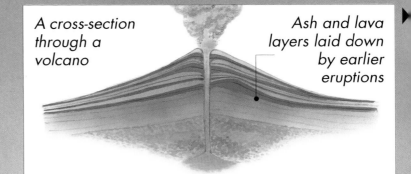

A cross-section through a volcano

Ash and lava layers laid down by earlier eruptions

A VOLCANO ERUPTS

A volcano is an opening in the Earth's crust—its rocky outer layer. (We usually think of a volcano as a cone-shaped mountain, but that is not always the case.) In a volcanic eruption, magma, hot melted rock from inside the Earth, is blasted out of the volcano's crater. It does this when gas that has built up inside the magma suddenly blows out. If the magma is thick and pasty, the eruption will be a very violent one. The erupted magma, called lava, is shattered into pumice and ash, forming a huge cloud. In lesser explosions, lava oozes from the crater and flows down the volcano's slopes.

Falling blocks of lava

Saiga galloping away from eruption

The year 500 BC

The Ice Ages have long been over. The summers in southern Italy are now warm and sunny. The soil is fertile and crops grow very well. Vesuvius lies close by. It has not erupted for many centuries. The people who live here have no idea that it is a dangerous volcano. To them it is simply a cone-shaped hill.

One day, this land will be part of the great Roman Empire, but at this time, it is under the rule of the Etruscans, a people of northern Italy.

Vesuvius

Italian pine tree

Farmhouse

Pigsty

Vines

VOLCANOES OF THE MEDITERRANEAN

The Earth's crust is like a jigsaw puzzle, divided into about 15 giant pieces scientists call "tectonic plates". These plates are always moving, although usually too slowly for us to notice. Most volcanoes are found on or near the edges of the plates (these are also the places where most earthquakes occur). Some plate edges lie beneath the Mediterranean Sea.

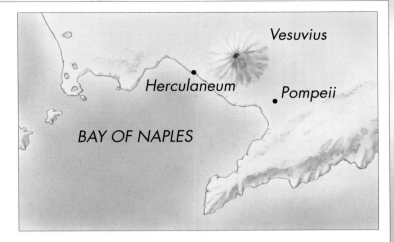

THE BAY OF NAPLES

Above is a map of the Bay of Naples. The crater of Vesuvius is clearly seen. The bay has good harbors for sea-going ships and the land is very fertile. For these reasons, this area has always had a large population. The towns of Pompeii and Herculaneum grew up near the southern slopes of Vesuvius.

25,000 years ago

500 BC

Etruscan temple

Plowing with oxen

24th August AD 79 10 am

It is a busy morning in the Roman town of Pompeii. In the square outside the Temple people gather to buy their groceries. Yet not everything seems to be right. Some of the animals are uneasy. A dog barks and strains at his leash.

A donkey upsets the cart he is pulling, and a caged bird flaps about in a panic.

A farmer from the slopes of Mount Vesuvius has felt a trembling underfoot and noticed an alarming bulge in the ground. He hurries down to Pompeii to report his fears to whomever will listen.

Vesuvius

Arch of Caligula

IMP · CAESAR · DIV · GERMANICVS

Writing messages

Drinks bar

Drawing water

THE ROMANS

In the first century AD, most of Mediterranean Europe was ruled by the Romans. Over many centuries Rome had grown from a small settlement on the banks of the Tiber River in Italy to the capital of a vast empire. The surrounding region became rich, able to trade in peace under the protection of the Roman army.

Prosperous towns such as Pompeii grew up close to the Bay of Naples, 120 miles to the southeast of Rome. A busy harbor brought in ships full of goods from overseas. Wealthy Pompeii merchants traded local produce—wine, cloth and *garum* (a fish sauce)—for glassware, jewels and spices. People crowded the town's bars, shops and taverns.

FORTVNAE

Temple of Fortuna Augusta

Butchers

Market stall

Guard

25,000 years ago

500 BC

24 Aug AD 79 10 am

This is what the eruption of Vesuvius would have looked like. The cloud of ash and pumice is shot high into the air before it spreads out.

Two hours later ...

Suddenly, there is a deafening explosion. Everyone in the square turns to look up at Vesuvius. People about to sit down to their midday meal indoors rush out onto the streets. Everyone stands and stares, spellbound by an amazing sight.

At just after noon, the build up of gases finally blew out the magma in Vesuvius' crater. The volcano erupted, blasting a column of pumice and ash (powdered volcanic rock) more than 12 miles straight up into the air.

Vesuvius

Arch of Caligula

IMP·CAESAR·DIV·GERMANICVS

People watching eruption

Shooting up into the air from the mountain's summit is a dense, black cloud. The people of Pompeii gasp in amazement. Few guessed that "their" mountain was actually a volcano. What they do not realize is that the eruption will soon put their lives in great danger. Some remember the great earthquake of 17 years earlier and wonder whether their houses will be damaged once again.

FORTVNAE AV

Temple of Fortuna Augusta

Market stall

Guard

25,000 years ago

500 BC

24 Aug AD 79 10 am

Two hours later

13

The cloud of pumice erupted from Vesuvius reached its maximum height after an hour. Winds then began to blow it in a south-easterly direction across Pompeii. The pumice then began to fall on the city.

One hour later ...

Pumice starts to rain down on Pompeii. The small fragments are too light to injure anyone seriously, but some people protect their heads all the same. The children discover pumice is good for sliding on, but some adults slip on it.

Vesuvius

Arch of Caligula

IMP · CAESAR · DIV · GERMANICVS ·

Head protection

Sliding on pumice

…e, the eruption continues.

…e cloud has now started to spread out …owards Pompeii. Some people who …watch the eruption from farther away …ater describe the shape of this cloud as …imilar to that of an Italian pine tree (see …page 8). The sky darkens and streaks of …lightning flash in the gathering gloom.

Pumice and ash settle on the ground. The fall will continue for 19 hours.

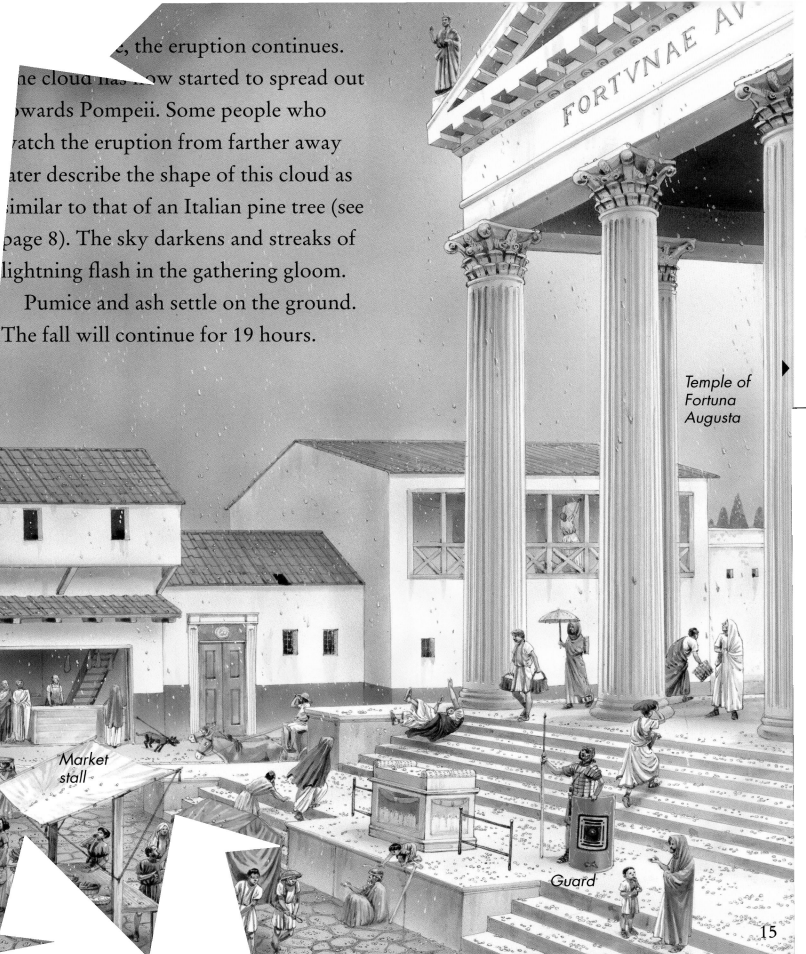

FORTVNAE AV

Temple of Fortuna Augusta

Market stall

Guard

25,000 years ago

500 BC

24 Aug AD 79 10 am

Two hours later

One hour later

15

This is what volcanic ash looks like under a microscope. The particles range in size from sand to flour. They are the remains of walls of "bubbles" inside the magma. These were caused by gas escaping from inside the liquid rock as it turned into pumice *(see page 7)*.

Later that afternoon...

The pumice and ash lie on the ground to a depth of three feet or so. Many roofs have started to collapse under the weight. People realize that their houses are in danger of falling down and that they are no longer safe indoors. Panic sets in.

Many people gather up their belongings, tie pillows to their heads to protect themselves from falling rocks and flee Pompeii. It is already too late to use a cart as the wheels become stuck in the pumice, so people carry what they can and trudge through the streets.

IMP·CAESAR·DIV·GERMANICVS

Arch of Caligula

People fleeing city

Cart stuck in pumice and ash

A dog, chained up and forgotten by its owner, barks wildly, straining at its leash. The guard, as instructed by his commanding officer, remains dutifully at his post.

Some people decide to stay. Many are too afraid to take to the streets. They pray to the gods that the dreadful fall of powdery rock will stop soon.

Roof collapsing under weight of pumice

Temple of Fortuna Augusta

Dog on leash

Pumice and ash lying thick on ground

Guard

25,000 years ago

500 BC

24 Aug AD 79 10 am

Two hours later

One hour later

Later that afternoon

17

This illustration shows the collapse of the column of ash and pumice, and the beginning of the pyroclastic flow that smothered Pompeii.

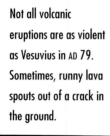

Not all volcanic eruptions are as violent as Vesuvius in AD 79. Sometimes, runny lava spouts out of a crack in the ground.

Early next morning...

The new day dawns in murky darkness. There is a loud explosion. A glowing red cloud rolls threateningly down the slopes of Vesuvius towards Pompeii. The few people that remain in the city look on in horror. What is this new danger?

Suddenly a blast of hot air knocks them off their feet. The force is so powerful it causes stone columns to crash to the ground. Soon afterwards, an avalanche of hot ash surges into the city, smashing almost everything in its path. Pompeii is destroyed.

Marble breaks off arch

Glowing cloud

Hot air blast knocks people over

GLOWING AVALANCHES

It was once thought that Pompeii was simply buried beneath layers of pumice and ash. Now there is evidence that avalanches of rock, glowing red-hot, surged down the slopes of Vesuvius and destroyed the city. Scientists call these avalanches *pyroclastic flows* (the word "pyroclastic" means "shattered by fire"). They happen when the great cloud of ash and pumice that blasts into the sky after a volcano erupts *(see page 12)* collapses back down to earth. Scientists studying a recent volcanic eruption (Mount St. Helens in Washington State, U.S., in 1980) discovered that a pyroclastic flow could travel at speeds of up to 180 miles per hour.

Temple collapsing

25,000 years ago

500 BC

24 Aug AD 79 10 am

Two hours later

One hour later

Later that afternoon

Early next morning

19

Because volcanic rock is so soft, it can be very easily dug out. This illustration shows the Rock Churches of Cappadocia in southern Turkey. The layers of ash, mud and lava created by ancient volcanic eruptions have been worn away over the centuries, leaving isolated "pillars". People discovered that the rock could be hollowed out to provide shelters. About a thousand years ago, many churches were dug out of the rocks.

During the eruption, Vesuvius really did "blow its top". The force of the explosion blasted apart the summit of the volcano. A vast new crater, measuring nearly a mile and a half across, was created.

One year later ...

Where there was once a city of 20,000 people, surrounded by fertile fields and vineyards, now there is a barren

Vesuvius

Ravine

landscape. Nothing grows here. The only people are curious visitors. Everywhere there is a thick layer of gray "snow", the ash and pumice that fell on Pompeii during the eruption of Vesuvius. It lies to a depth of between three and five yards, completely covering the ruins of the Roman city.

Each time it rains, torrential streams flow, gouging out ravines in the soft material. A few bare tree stumps stick out from the ash layers.

Yet within a few years, the countryside will be rich and green once more. Volcanic soils are very fertile, and plants and flowers soon burst into life.

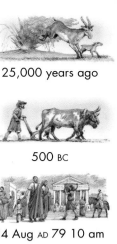
25,000 years ago

500 BC

24 Aug AD 79 10 am

Two hours later

One hour later

Later that afternoon

Early next morning

One year later

Barren, ash-covered ground

Ravine

Hunting party

Tree stumps

21

The illustrations show how the shape of Vesuvius has changed over the centuries. The first *(above)* shows what it probably looked like just before the AD 79 eruption.

This is the crater of Vesuvius immediately after the eruption. The summit has been blown off by the explosion.

Today, a new cone has formed on the south side of the old crater. It has erupted many times since AD 79.

Volcanoes grow out of the ground. Sometimes they can reach a great height in just a few years. On Vesuvius, a new volcanic cone began to grow over the centuries. There was still magma beneath it.

More than a thousand years later ...

Lying under its thick blanket of volcanic ash and pumice, Pompeii has been buried and forgotten for many years. The Roman Empire also ended

Vesuvius

Finding broken tiles

Gold coin

many centuries ago, and no new cities have grown up in this area. Instead, country people plow the land and graze their livestock. The fertile volcanic soils ensure that their farms are prosperous, and they live good lives.

Sometimes, coins, tiles, pieces of pottery or old columns are dug up, but no one thinks anything of them.

THE STORY OF VESUVIUS

Vesuvius has erupted about 80 times since AD 79, although rarely with such devastating violence. The worst eruption was in 1631, when 4000 people were killed. Glowing avalanches were, once again, the cause of this disaster.

The last time Vesuvius erupted was in 1944. Since then, it has been dormant (a period of inactivity between eruptions). No one knows when it might erupt again, or how powerful that eruption might be.

A volcano that has stopped erupting altogether is described as extinct. Since there may be many hundreds of years between eruptions, it is often hard to decide whether a volcano is extinct or not.

25,000 years ago

500 BC

24 Aug AD 79 10 am

Two hours later

One hour later

Later that afternoon

Early next morning

One year later

1250

Old column

The discovery of the lost cities of Pompeii and Herculaneum began with finds of pieces of marble with inscriptions carved on them. Here, a peasant comes across such a find while digging a well in the ground. Some earlier discoveries that even had the name of Pompeii inscribed on them were ignored.

The ruins of Pompeii were fascinating to many artists. Soon after Pompeii was found, some made accurate drawings of the remains.

The year 1785

Wealthy people from all over Europe visit the ruins of Pompeii. Ever since the news broke that an ancient city had been discovered under the ground near Vesuvius, travelers have been eager to see the remains for themselves.

Some of Pompeii's visitors are treasure hunters, with wheelbarrows and spades. Pieces of marble are broken off and taken away as souvenirs.

Vesuvius

Digging for treasure

Columns, vases, statues and wall paintings are dug up and taken away. Some discoveries are used as ornaments. Others are put on display in museums.

But other people come to study the ruins in order to find out about the past. They make drawings, and try to imagine what Pompeii's buildings would have looked like before they were destroyed.

THE DISCOVERY OF POMPEII

The lost city of Pompeii remained forgotten for many centuries. Even after the ruins of buildings, statues and wall paintings were discovered by workmen building a tunnel in 1594, nobody was interested. In 1710 a peasant digging a well a few miles from where Pompeii once stood found several slabs of marble buried deep in the ground. Then a local nobleman guessed that other treasures might be found there and bought the land. The remains of old houses were dug up and Herculaneum, another town destroyed in the AD 79 eruption of Vesuvius, was soon discovered. It was not long before people came across the ruins of Pompeii. Digging began in 1748.

25,000 years ago

500 BC

24 Aug AD 79 10 am

Two hours later

One hour later

Later that afternoon

Early next morning

One year later

1250

1785

Finding a statue

Column

25

These three illustrations show how Fiorelli made plaster casts of dead people and animals found at Pompeii. In the first illustration *(above)*, a woman is buried by falling ash and pumice.

The layers of ash and pumice set hard around her body. This later rots away, leaving a body-shaped hollow. Fiorelli filled the hollow with liquid plaster.

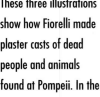

After the plaster had set, Fiorelli dug away the ash, leaving a perfect cast of the body that once filled the hollow. Nowadays, casts are made using a tough, transparent material so we can see the bones inside.

A hundred years later ...

Thanks to the efforts of hundreds of workers armed with picks and shovels, the ruins of Pompeii are gradually emerging from the deep layers of pumice and ash that have covered them over for so long. An archaeologist named Giuseppe Fiorelli has been appointed to supervise the excavation of Pompeii. He has made sure that proper scientific records are made of Pompeii's ruins.

First of all, mounds of ash are cleared away. He divides up the site into regions.

Arch of Caligula *(brick arch stripped of marble)*

Vesuvius

Carrying away rubble in baskets

Removing ash

Supervisor

Photographer

Every block and building inside each region is given a number. This means that whenever an object is found, its precise position can be recorded. Now scientists can find out much more about how people lived in Roman times.

Teams of workers (some are convicts) carry away pumice and ash in straw baskets, watched over by supervisors. They make sure nothing is stolen. Other workers are busy making plaster casts of dead people whose skeletons have been found. They were the unfortunate ones who could not escape the glowing avalanches that engulfed Pompeii (see page 18). The layers of volcanic ash that covered them over quickly hardened. In time, the flesh and clothing rotted away, leaving body-shaped hollows in the ash. Giuseppe Fiorelli invented a way of making copies of the bodies by pouring plaster into these hollows.

25,000 years ago

500 BC

24 Aug AD 79 10 am

Two hours later

One hour later

Later that afternoon

Early next morning

One year later

1250

1785

100 years later

Supervisor

Artist

Making plaster casts

Statue

The finds made at Pompeii tell us a great deal about life in Roman times. By being buried in ash, even some foods have survived to the present day.

Fiorelli's method of making plaster casts was also used for animals. This dog was buried alive, struggling to free itself of its chain.

Contests between gladiators were popular in Roman times. There was an amphitheatre (a kind of stadium) in Pompeii where such contests took place. Wall paintings, plaster casts of gladiators' bodies and finds of helmets and armor tell us what the contests were like.

Today

Visitors flock to see the ruins of Pompeii (about two million come each year). There are guides on hand to make sure that people can find their way around the streets. They also answer questions about, for example, what life was like in Pompeii before it was destroyed, what happened during the eruption of Vesuvius and how the ruins were discovered and restored for all to see.

The ruins of ancient Pompeii are very old and need to be looked after carefully.

Vesuvius

Arch of Caligula

Guide

Well

At the mercy of the weather and pollution, the crumbling walls are at risk from falling into a worse condition.

Many of Pompeii's tall buildings were knocked down by the great force of the glowing avalanches (see page 18). Some of those that have remained standing were plundered for building stone a long time ago. As a result, tall buildings are quite rare in Pompeii, although the great Arch of Caligula still stands proudly.

The tourists admire the many wonderful sights Pompeii still boasts. They stroll around its streets enjoying the warm, sunny weather. Some wonder what it would have been like to live and work in Pompeii when it was a bustling Roman town nearly 2000 years ago.

Have you noticed how some people in this scene remind you of characters that appeared here in Roman times? Take a close look on pages 10 and 11!

25,000 years ago

500 BC

24 Aug AD 79 10 am

Two hours later

One hour later

Later that afternoon

Early next morning

One year later

1250

1785

100 years later

Today

Kiosk

Ruins of Temple of Fortuna Augusta

Guard

Glossary

Active volcano A volcano that is erupting.

Amphitheatre In Roman times, an oval-shaped building used for gladiatorial contests. It had a central arena surrounded by rows of seats rising above it.

Archaeologist Someone who studies human life from the past, using the evidence from finds buried in the ground or at sea.

Ash, volcanic Lava that has been blown to powder by the force of the explosion when a volcano erupts.

Crater The circular, funnel-shaped basin at the summit of a volcanic cone.

Dormant volcano A volcano that has stopped erupting, but which may burst into life again in the future.

Earthquake A shaking or trembling of the ground, caused by the sudden movement of part of the Earth's crust. Earthquakes usually (but not always) occur near the boundaries of tectonic plates.

Eruption The blasting out of lava, ash or pumice from a volcano into the air or onto the Earth's surface.

Excavation The unearthing of buried objects in an attempt to find out about the past.

Extinct volcano A volcano that has permanently stopped erupting.

Gladiators In Roman times, men trained to fight in an amphitheatre for public entertainment.

Ice Age A cold period in the Earth's history when ice spread out from the poles and mountain ranges to cover large areas of the Earth's surface. The last Ice Age began about 2 million years ago and may not have ended yet.

Inscriptions Writing carved on wood, stone or metal.

Lava Magma that has erupted onto the Earth's surface through volcanoes.

Magma Hot, melted (molten) rock that comes from beneath the solid rock of the Earth's crust.

Plaster cast A copy or mold of a person, animal or object made from plaster of Paris, a white powder that becomes solid when mixed with water.

Pumice A volcanic glass "froth" formed from cooling gassy lava. It contains many bubbles.

Pyroclastic flow Hot, glowing avalanches of lava fragments that surge down the slopes of a volcano during an eruption.

Ravine A deep, narrow valley formed by the action of a fast-running stream.

Tectonic plates The large slabs into which the Earth's surface is divided. Each plate moves slowly, either pushing into another plate, sliding underneath it, or pulling away from it. Many volcanoes are located at or near the plate boundaries.

Volcano An opening in the Earth's crust through which magma erupts. The term is normally used to describe a cone-shaped mountain with a crater at its summit.